Ride Directory

Number

Ride Name

Rides are listed in order of difficulty from easiest to hardest

Page

DEDICATED TO BURNEY FAIR. SHE RODE LIKE SHE LIVED, WITH LOVE AND PASSION AND NO BRAKES.

Thanks go to the following people whose help made this book possible: First and foremost, my parents, Robert and Myra Rich for their encouragement, advice and editing; Doug Berry for his great photos; Daiva Chesonis/Vision Design for her design work; Editors and proofreaders: Geoff Shaffer and C.J. Davis. Also, thanks to Trails Illustrated, the U.S. Forest Service, Jefferson County Open Space Parks, Boulder County Parks and Open Space and Lakewood Parks Department for the use of their maps.

Special Thanks To  Cycle Computers

To order more books or address questions, comments, and suggestions, write to Little Rose Publishing, Box 884, Telluride, CO 81435.

Introduction

The mountains surrounding Boulder are criss-crossed with enough trails and roads to keep any rider busy for a long time, even though many trails near town have been closed to bikers. Boulderides offers trails for all ability levels from the absolute beginner to the most hard-core expert. There are gently rolling dirt roads; white-knuckle descents; and gonzo/technical trails all within 45 minutes of town.

Riding around Boulder can be a trip into history. The area is dotted with abandoned mines, ghost towns, and forgotten homesteads that tell of Boulder's founding and remind us why people settled in this spectacular mountain environment.

Entering the backcountry entails a certain responsibility on each rider's part to ensure that it remains in its pristine state. Mountain bikers are, increasingly, criticized by various groups for their impact on the terrain. It is crucial that each of us does his or her part to preserve the integrity of the environment. As the bumper sticker says: Love it or leave it alone.

Each ride is described in ten ways: round trip length in miles, ride time, elevation gain, high point, physical and technical difficulty, type of terrain, access, a detailed description of the route, and trail notes. To determine length and elevation gain I used a cycle computer with an altimeter and verified these figures with a topographic map. Ride time is an estimated range with the low-end representing the length of time it would take a racer or someone in comparable shape and the high-end representing a less experienced or less conditioned rider's time. Ride time takes into account the difficulty of a route and I have assumed that, in general, beginners would not attempt a ride like the Maverick Trail. The difficulty of each ride is determined by comparing each to the others and then rating it by its physical and technical difficulty. Although the two are related, physical difficulty is pretty much sheer exertion, while technical difficulty is a rating of the number and type of obstacles to overcome. These might include stream crossings, rocky climbs and descents, and sections of trail that require advanced skills to maneuver through, such as a steep, tight, switchbacking section. I used the ski area rating system to symbolize the difficulty of each ride.

● The easiest trail, pretty much anyone can do it.

●● Some sustained climbs or mild technical sections.

■ For people who have mountain biking experience or are in relatively good shape.

■■ For intermediate-level bikers who are in very good shape and acclimated to the altitude.

◆ For advanced, experienced riders in very good to excellent condition.

◆◆ Combination of extreme terrain and/or altitude make this for Experts Only!

Because mountain bicycling is an intensely aerobic sport, I'd recommend that you start with a ride at or below what you consider to be your level and progress from there.

Trail Rules

1 **Stay on the Trail** At high altitude the ecosystem is fragile, easily damaged and takes years to heal.

2 **Pack Out At Least As Much As You Pack In.**

3 **Leave Gates as You Find Them.**

4 **Never Startle Animals** Stop and let animals move away from the trail, then pass slowly.

5 **Yield The Trail** Let other trail users know you are approaching. Yield to hikers and uphill riding bikers. Horses are easily scared by bikes. Always stop, move off the trail and let them pass.

6 **Always Ride in Control.**

7 **Respect Closed Areas** Do not trespass on private lands, or ride on closed trails or in wilderness areas. If you are not sure a trail is open, ask first!

Essentials

1 **Always Wear A Helmet.**

2 **Altitude Sickness** can be a serious problem. Give yourself a chance to acclimate and do not over-exert during your first few days at high altitude. Drink plenty of water; this will help a lot! Symptoms of altitude sickness include nausea, dizziness and headaches. The best remedy, if possible, is to return to a lower elevation as quickly as possible.

3 **Do Not Drink Untreated Water Out Of Any Stream or Lake! Giardia is Common in Untreated Water.**

4 **Food and Drink** Bring two liters of water per person. Food isn't a necessity but you'll be glad to have some. Good biking snacks include energy bars, trail mix, apples and anything else that is easily digested and high in carbohydrates.

5 **Clothing** The main idea is Be Prepared! The weather changes rapidly in the mountains. Getting caught in a storm at 10,000 feet is not only unpleasant, but can be dangerous as well. Hypothermia is a threat, even in summer and it can snow any month of the year. Always bring a good raincoat and an extra shirt. Biking gloves are a plus: they protect your hands in a fall and absorb vibration during rough descents. Other musts at altitude are sunscreen and sunglasses; The sun is much more intense at high altitude (Every 1,000 feet gained in elevation increases exposure to harmful rays by 4%). Sunglasses also provide good eye protection.

6 **Tools** Each group of riders should have a pump, patch kit or spare tube, chain tool, 4, 5, 6 mm allen wrenches, tire irons, a phillips head screwdriver, and an 8, 9 and 10 mm wrench. If you are going into the backcountry, a first aid kit is always a good idea.

7 **Maintenance** Always check over your bike before riding, or have a bike mechanic do it if you are unfamiliar with bikes.

4

Distance	**9 miles**
Time	**.45-1.5 hours**
Elevation Gain	**800 ft**
High Point	**8,450 ft**
Physical Difficulty	●
Technical Difficulty	●
Terrain	**Paved Road, Dirt Road**

Access from Canyon and Broadway Drive west on Canyon (Hwy 119) to Nederland, bear left on Hwy 119 and take the first right into the public parking lot.
Drive Time 25 minutes

The Ride Turn left out of the lot onto Hwy 72 East, toward Ward. Ride 2.5 miles up the paved road and turn right on Cold Springs Road. Descend and climb along this pretty aspen and pine tree-lined road. At 4.4 miles, bear left and continue climbing to the end of the dirt road. At 5 miles, turn right on the paved Cold Springs Road. Stay right at Hurricane Hill and descend to Hwy 72. Turn left and return to Nederland.

Trail Notes Cold Springs Road is an excellent beginner ride. The first climb, up Hwy 72, is the toughest. The dirt road sections are not technical and are lightly traveled. The highway will have some fast moving traffic, but Boulder-area drivers are generally considerate of cyclists.

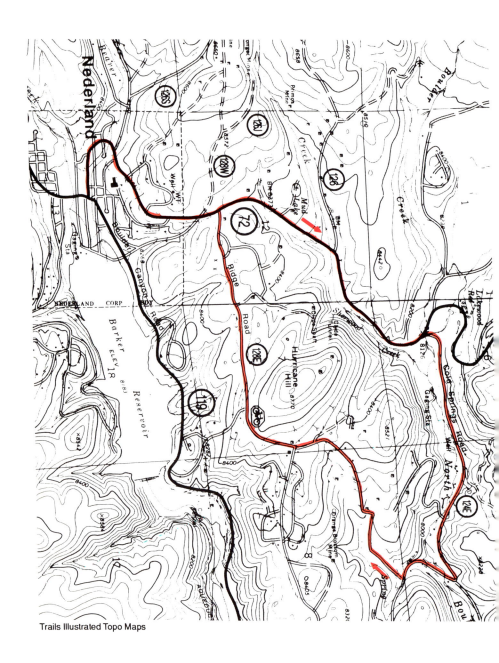

Trails Illustrated Topo Maps

6

2 Magnolia Road

Distance	16 miles
Time	1.5-2.5 hours
Elevation Gain	860 ft
High Point	8,700 ft
Physical Difficulty	●●
Technical Difficulty	●
Terrain	Dirt Road

Access from Canyon and Broadway Ride or drive 5 miles west on Canyon (Hwy 119). Just past a tunnel, turn left on the signed Magnolia Road. Climb this very steep, paved road for 4.7 miles to the end of the pavement and park off the road.
Drive Time 20 minutes

The Ride Following the main road at all junctions, pedal along this easy dirt road to its end at Hwy 119 above Nederland. The road neither climbs nor descends too steeply or for too long at any point. On the way back, be sure to bear left at a junction with a Forest Service road. It's an obvious turn, but the two roads do look alike.

Trail Notes This is a great beginner ride because it is neither technically nor physically challenging. The road is very pleasant, generally lightly traveled and not very dusty. There are views of the Indian Peaks in places and pine trees line most of this sunny route. The first 4.7 miles on pavement climb nearly 2,000 feet and provide an awesome workout if you pedal instead of drive.

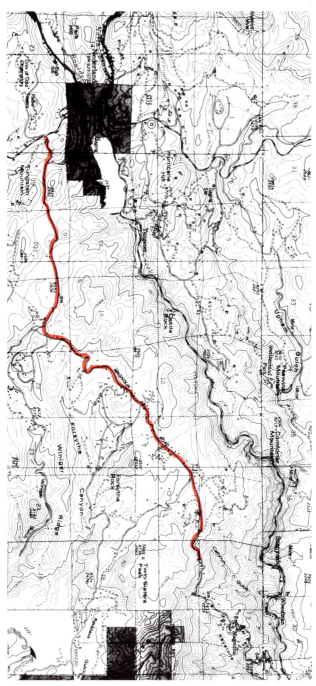

Trails Illustrated Topo Maps

3 **Moffat Tunnel**

Distance	**17 miles**
Time	**1.5-2.5 hours**
Elevation Gain	**700 ft**
High Point	**9,210 ft**
Physical Difficulty	●●
Technical Difficulty	●
Terrain	**Dirt Road**

Access from Canyon and Broadway Drive west on Canyon (Hwy 119) to Nederland, bear left, continuing on 119 West, and drive 5 miles to Rollinsville. In Rollinsville, turn right on Road 16, following the signs for Rollins Pass and the Moffat Tunnel. Park off the road, about 100 yards up, just past several buildings and houses.
Drive Time 35 minutes

The Ride Follow Rollins Pass Road as it climbs gradually up the South Boulder Creek valley. Pass Tolland and stay straight at a fork for Apex. Continue up the road, cross a set of train tracks, stay straight at a junction for Rollins Pass and end at the Moffat Tunnel. Return as you came.

Trail Notes The Rollins Pass road is a mellow ride with nice views. It does get a fair amount of auto traffic and the road can be dusty. It's best when there hasn't been a long stretch of dry weather.

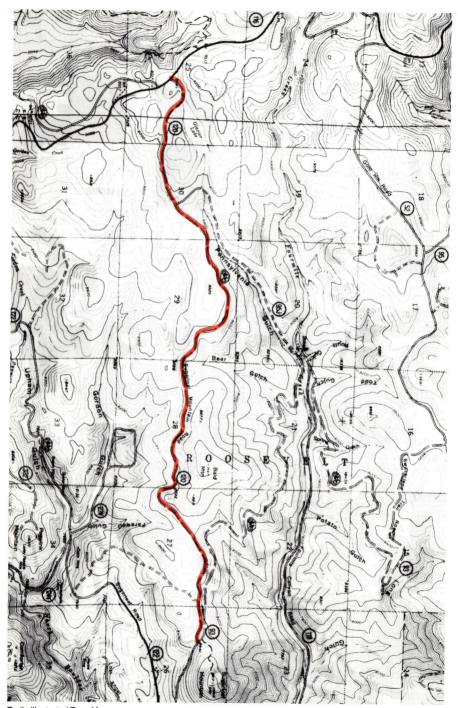

Trails Illustrated Topo Maps

12

5 / Elem School Loop

```
E
L
E   9000
V   8500
A   8000
T      0  1  2  3  4  5  6
I
O        M  I  L  E  S
N
```

Distance	5.6 miles
Time	45-1.5 hours
Elevation Gain	550 ft
High Point	8,800 ft
Physical Difficulty	●●
Technical Difficult	●●
Terrain	2WD Road

Access from Canyon and Broadway Drive west on Canyon (Hwy 119) to Nederland, turn left on 119 and take your first right into the public parking lot.
Drive Time 25 minutes

The Ride Turn left out of the parking lot onto Hwy 72 East, toward Ward. Ride 1.1 miles up this paved road and turn left at a sign for Elem School. The road forks immediately. Stay right and climb .3 miles. Stay right and uphill at another junction and continue .6 miles until the road ends at an improved dirt road. Turn right and then take your first left on Rd 108. Descend to the highway, turn right and ride back to Nederland.

Trail Notes This easy road loops above Nederland, climbing gradually to an intersection with the Caribou Road. Nederland was named by miners working at the Caribou mill. The name comes from the Dutch word Ned, meaning low lands, because at 8,235 feet, Nederland is dwarfed by Caribou, perched at 10,000 feet. Nederland was founded in 1871 to serve the huge silver mill at Caribou. Since then, the town's fortunes have risen and fallen with the discoveries of silver in 1870 at Caribou, gold in the 1880s, and then white gold or snow in the 1960s at Eldora. In between, Nederland has often teetered on the brink of becoming a ghost town, though today tourist traffic from Boulder has stabilized its economy.

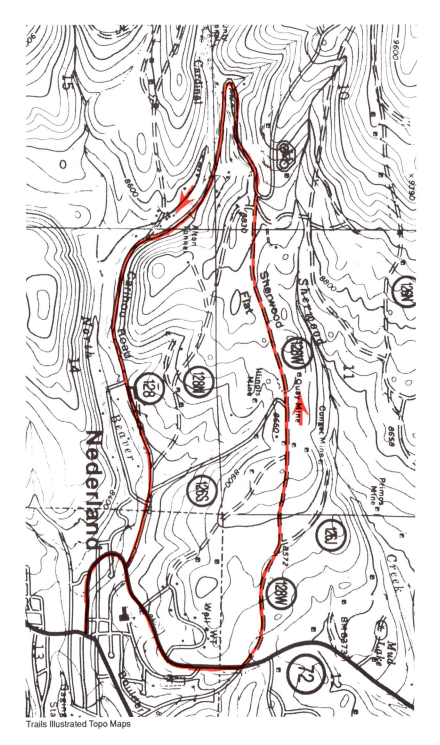

Trails Illustrated Topo Maps

14

6 Ward to Gold Hill

Distance	16.6 miles
Time	2-4 hours
Elevation Gain	1,000 ft
High Point	9,550 ft
Physical Difficulty	■
Technical Difficulty	●
Terrain	Dirt Road

ELEVATION

10000
9500
9000
8500

0 1 2 3 4 5 6 7 8 9 10 11 12 13 14 15 16 17

M I L E S

Access from Canyon and Broadway Drive 17 miles west on Canyon (Hwy 119) to Nederland, turn right on Highway 72 East and continue 12.5 miles to Ward. Turn right into Ward and park off the road.
Drive Time 40 minutes

The Ride From Ward, ride 1.3 miles on Left Hand Canyon Drive and turn right at the first fork on the dirt Sawmill Road. Climb a short, steep hill and continue 1.2 miles before intersecting the Gold Hill Road. Turn left and coast to Gold Hill. Turn right at a stop sign and end in front of the Gold Hill General Store. Return as you came.

Option 1 One option on the return trip from Gold Hill is the Switzerland Trail, a non-demanding railroad grade. To access it, turn right on the signed trail, 2.6 miles from Gold Hill. The trail winds along the mountain side for 3.5 miles without gaining or losing much altitude. The trail ends on a scree field, but Sawmill Road is just a brief scramble above you and the paved Left Hand Canyon Drive is visible below. After climbing up to Sawmill Road, turn downhill on it, ride to its end at Left Hand Canyon Drive, turn left and return to Ward.

Trail Notes This is an easy ride along a fairly lightly traveled dirt road between two former mining camps. There is still motor vehicle traffic along it; be on the lookout for cars.

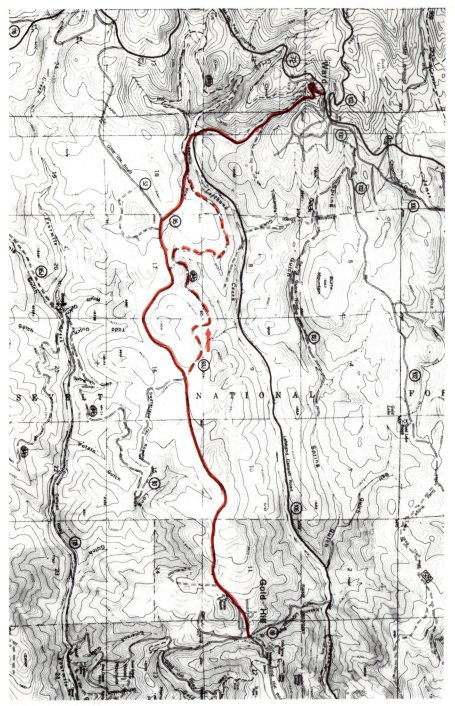

Trails Illustrated Topo Maps

16

7 **Gold Lake Road**

Distance	6.6 miles
Time	1-2 hours
Elevation Gain	600 ft
High Point	9,260 ft
Physical Difficulty	■
Technical Difficulty	●●
Terrain	2WD Road

ELEVATION

9500
9000
8500

0 1 2 3 4 5 6 7

M I L E S

Access from Canyon and Broadway Drive west on Canyon (Hwy 119) to Nederland. Turn right on Hwy 72 East and drive 12 miles to Ward. Gold Lake Road is just past Ward on the right side of the road. Park in a pull-off next to it.
Drive Time 40 minutes

The Ride Descend .3 miles on Gold Lake Road to a junction and turn right. Continue descending, staying straight on the main road at all junctions. The road ends at Gold Lake. Return as you came.

Trail Notes This easy road leads to a lake with views to the Front Range. Gold Lake Road is a public access, but the land on both sides of the road, including the lake, is private. Please don't trespass.

17

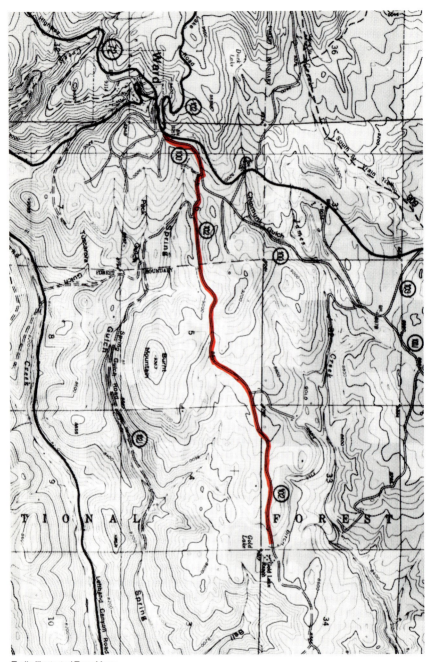

Trails Illustrated Topo Maps

18

8 Sugarloaf Loop

Distance	**15.5 miles**
Time	**2-4 hours**
Elevation Gain	**1,300 ft**
High Point	**9,100 ft**
Physical Difficulty	■
Technical Difficulty	■
Terrain	**2WD Road,**
	Paved Road

Access from Canyon and Broadway Ride or drive 5.4 miles west on Canyon (Hwy 119) toward Nederland. Shortly after passing through a tunnel, turn right on Sugarloaf Road (5.4 miles from Boulder) and go 5 miles to Sugar Mtn. Road. Turn right and continue .9 miles to the trail-head parking.
Drive Time 20 minutes

The Ride From the Switzerland Trail parking, take the left-hand road with a sign pointing to Glacier Lake. Follow this road, staying on it at all junctions, to its end at the Peak to Peak Hwy (Hwy 72). Carefully cross the highway and join the dirt road on the other side (CR 103). Descend 3 miles to its end back at the Peak to Peak. Turn right on the highway, ride .1 miles and take your first left on the Sugarloaf road (BC 122). Climb, descend and climb again until you intersect Sugar Mountain Road, soon after the road turns from dirt to asphalt. Turn left and climb steeply for 1 mile back to the start.

Trail Notes This is a fun loop for beginner and intermediate riders following several non-technical dirt roads. There is little vehicle traffic to contend with, except on the Sugarloaf road. Views of the Indian Peaks abound on the backstretch of the loop.

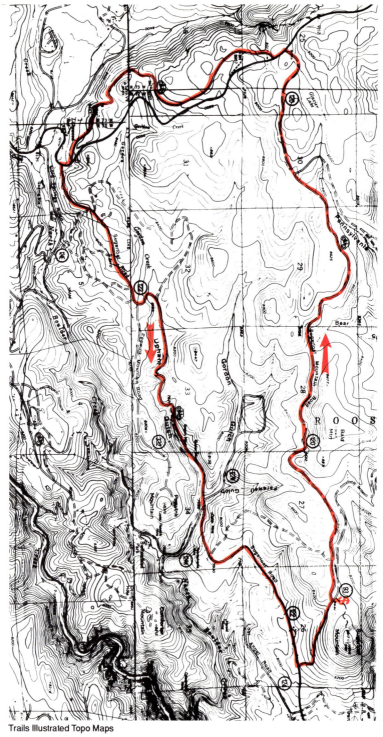

Trails Illustrated Topo Maps

20

9 Gold Hill Loop

Distance	**25.4 miles**
Time	**2.5-4 hours**
Elevation Gain	**1,700 ft**
High Point	**8,700 ft**
Physical Difficulty	■
Technical Difficulty	●●
Terrain	**2WD Road,**
	Paved, Dirt Road

Access from Canyon and Broadway Ride or drive 5.4 miles west on Canyon (Hwy 119) toward Nederland. Shortly after passing through a tunnel, turn right on Sugarloaf Road (5.4 miles from Boulder) and go 5 miles to Sugar Mtn. Road. Turn right and continue .9 miles to the trailhead parking.
Drive Time 20 minutes

The Ride From the parking lot, take the right-hand road, following the signs to Sunset. The first part of the ride is a rocky, bumpy 4 mile descent most bikers should be able to handle easily. When you reach the town of Sunset, turn right on CR 118, at its junction with FS109. The green sign for 118 is about 100 yards down the road. Coast downhill for almost 6 miles, past Wall Street to Salina, where you intersect the paved Four Mile Canyon Road. Turn left, following the signs to Gold Hill and begin a 4 mile climb. The first 2 miles are the toughest. Stay straight at an intersection with lots of mail boxes lining the right side of the road and continue to Gold Hill. Take your second left at the stop sign, ride past the general store and turn left at a small wooden sign pointing to Ward. Climb briefly, before descending to an intersection with the Switzerland Trail. Turn left on the Switzerland Trail and follow it as it descends to Sunset. Go straight through Sunset on FS109 and climb back to the start on Sugar Loaf.

Trail Notes The Gold Hill Loop is a long but relatively non-strenuous and non-technical ride on lightly traveled roads. It's a great tour for intermediate riders in good shape or stronger riders looking to get out and spin.

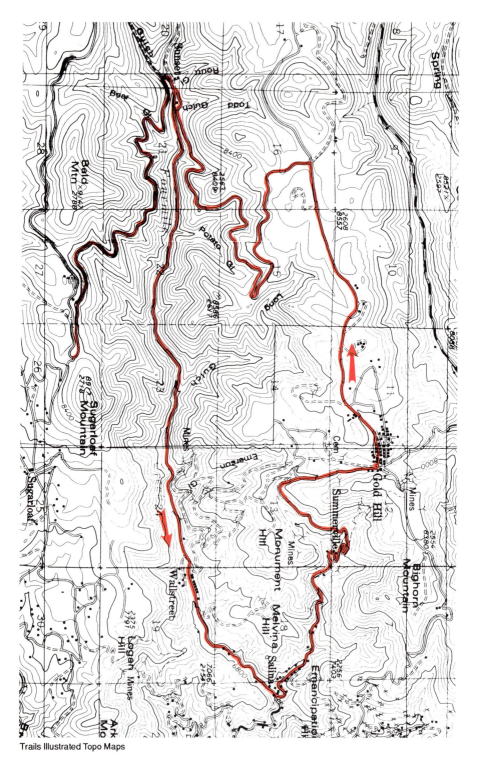

10 Switzerland Trail

Distance	**24.8 miles**
Time	**2.5-4 hours**
Elevation Gain	**1,800 ft**
High Point	**8,600 ft**
Physical Difficulty	■
Technical Difficulty	■
Terrain	**2WD Road**

Access from Canyon and Broadway Ride or drive west on Canyon (Hwy 119) toward Nederland. Shortly after passing through a tunnel, turn right on the signed Sugarloaf Road (5.4 miles from Boulder). Drive 5 miles to Sugar Mtn. Road, turn right and continue .9 miles to the trail-head parking.
Drive Time 20 minutes

The Ride Begin by following the road on the right side of the parking area with a sign pointing to Sunset. Descend, staying straight on the rocky, main road at all intersections. At the bottom of the first hill, stay right at a junction with a 4WD road and come to the town of Sunset. Go straight on FS 109 at a junction with CR 118. Begin a long, but not too tiring climb, looping around Bald Mountain. Pass a picnic area and inter-sect Gold Hill Road at 8.7 miles. Turn right and descend to a stop sign above the town of Gold Hill. Turn right again and end at the General Store in town. Return as you came.

Trail Notes The Switzerland Trail was constructed in 1881 for the nar-row gauge railroad to run gold ore from the mines around Sugarloaf and Gold Hill to the mill in Boulder. In 1919, soon after the mines were shut down, the tracks were pulled up leaving behind a gentle grade which is ideal for biking. There is only one slightly technical section, a rocky downhill on the return trip from Gold Hill, so beginner in good shape could enjoy it. The trail also makes a fantastic training ride for someone looking for a good workout. You can get out and spin a big gear for many miles. Bring some money to buy a snack at the Gold Hill General Store before making the return trip.

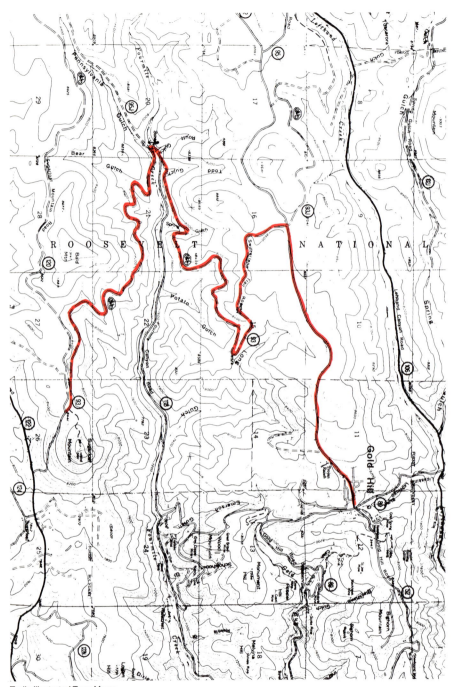

Trails Illustrated Topo Maps

11 Rollins Pass

Distance	29 miles
Time	3-5 hours
Elevation Gain	2,600 ft
High Point	11,670 ft
Physical Difficulty	■■
Technical Difficulty	■
Terrain	2WD Road

ELEVATION

MILES

Access from Canyon and Broadway Take Hwy 119 (Canyon) west to Nederland. Turn left in Nederland on Hwy 119 and continue 5 miles to Rollinsville. Turn right on the Rollins Pass Road (CR 16) and drive for 7.5 miles to the bottom of Rollins Pass, a signed right turn near the Moffat Tunnel.
Drive Time 45 minutes

The Ride Rollins Pass was originally a railroad grade and thus climbs gradually all the way to the top. Stay on the main road at all junctions. At 10 miles, pass Yankee Doodle Lake. Above the lake you will have to portage around the Needle Eye Tunnel, which was condemned after part of it collapsed on a car. Continue climbing to the top of the pass and return as you came.

Trail Notes The Rollins Pass Road is not especially strenuous but is very long. The summit of the pass is at 11,670 feet so low-altitude folk should be acclimated before attempting this ride. Be prepared for changing weather conditions as you will be exposed high above tree line and shelter is far below.

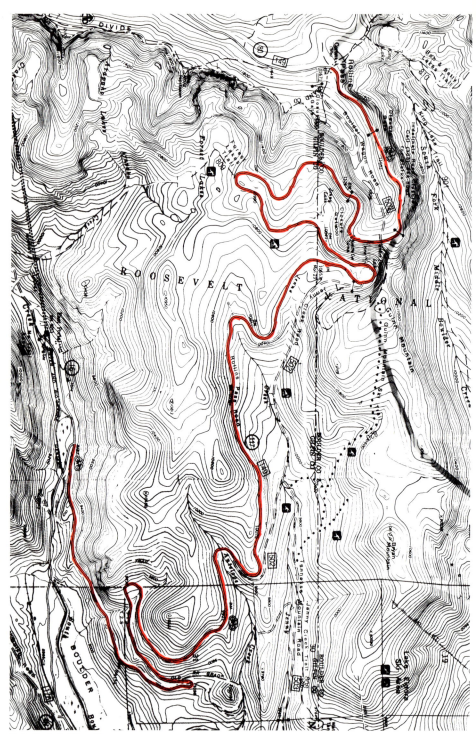

Trails Illustrated Topo Maps

Distance	6.9 miles
Time	1-2 hours
Elevation Gain	950 ft
High Point	6,750 ft
Physical Difficulty	■
Technical Difficulty	■■
Terrain	**Trail**

Access from Canyon and Broadway Drive south on Broadway to the intersection of Hwy 93 and Hwy 6, at a traffic light in Golden. Bear left and then turn right at the second traffic light you come to, which is Jefferson County Parkway (23.3 miles from Boulder). Follow the signs for Morrison and I-70, drive under I-70 and continue downhill 1.4 miles to an intersection with Hwy 26 East. Turn left, climb up and over the Hogback and turn left again at the bottom of the hill on Rooney Road. Drive .7 miles and turn right into the Green Mtn. parking lot.
Drive Time 40 minutes

The Ride Ride over the highway on a bridge and join a dirt road on the other side. Go straight on the dirt road and begin climbing, bearing left and circling clockwise around Green Mountain. At the top of the climb are great views of Denver. Pass one trail, descend and climb briefly on the dirt road, and turn right on a single track. Follow this narrow trail downhill. Stay right at an intersection with a second trail and negotiate several switchbacks. At an intersection at the bottom of the descent, bear right on the uphill trail and follow this rollercoastering path as it continues around Green Mtn. Pass several dirt roads but remain on the trail at all of these. Climb one last small hill, bear left and return to the start.

Trail Notes Green Mountain Trail is a good introduction to single track riding for someone who's starting to really get into the sport and has some bike handling skills. The trail combines moderate climbs with a few technical challenges. The Green Mtn. Trail is uncrowded compared with other Front Range rides. It is popular with hikers; ride in control and be prepared to yield to other trail users. In early summer, Green Mountain is covered with an amazing carpet of red, blue, violet and yellow wild flowers; it's beautiful!

27

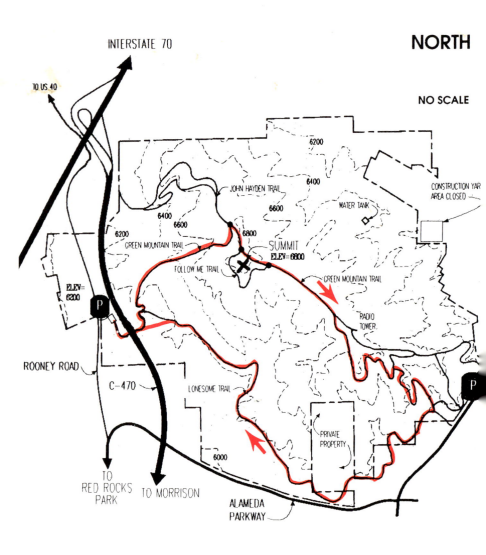

INTERSTATE 70

NORTH

NO SCALE

TO US 40

6200

6400

JOHN HAYDEN TRAIL

WATER TANK

CONSTRUCTION YAR
AREA CLOSED

6400
6600

6600

6800

6200

GREEN MOUNTAIN TRAIL

SUMMIT
ELEV=6800

FOLLOW ME TRAIL

GREEN MOUNTAIN TRAIL

ELEV=
6200

P

RADIO
TOWER

ROONEY ROAD

C-470

LONESOME TRAIL

P

PRIVATE
PROPERTY

6000

TO
RED ROCKS
PARK

TO MORRISON

ALAMEDA
PARKWAY

28

13 **Sourdough Trail**
Brainard Lake

Distance	**12 miles**
Time	**2.5-4 hours**
Elevation Gain	**1,550 ft**
High Point	**10,550 ft**
Physical Difficulty	■■
Technical Difficulty	■■
Terrain	**Trail**

ELEVATION

11000
10500
10000
9500

0 1 2 3 4 5 6 7 8 9 10 11 12

M I L E S

Access from Canyon and Broadway Drive west on Canyon (Hwy 119) to Nederland and turn right on Hwy 72 East toward Ward. Drive 7.5 miles and turn left on the C.U. Research Station road (FS 298). Continue .4 miles to the Sourdough trailhead and park off the road.
Drive Time 40 minutes

The Ride Begin by climbing rather steeply through a section of dense pine forest. The trail is well marked at every intersection. Cross a bridge and continue climbing. The top of the climb is at 10,500 feet; be prepared for variable conditions (we hit snow in early June and October). From the top of the trail, descend to the paved Brainard Lake road and return the way you came.

Trail Notes The Sourdough Trail is one of the nicest single tracks in Boulder County. When many other trails in the area turn sandy toward the end of summer, the Sourdough is still hard packed dirt because it's shaded and at high altitude. The trail offers enough technical challenge for the advanced rider, while remaining fun for the intermediate. There are views toward the plains in the few places where there are breaks in the otherwise dense forest.

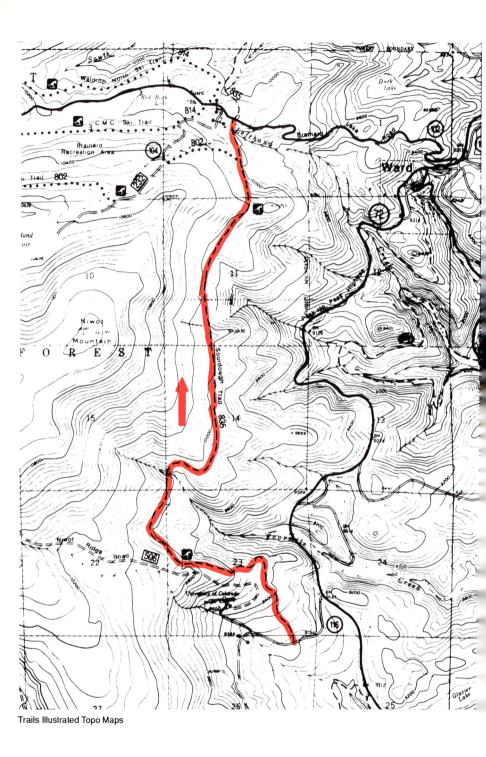

Trails Illustrated Topo Maps

30

14 Apex Park

Distance	**5.6 miles**
Time	**1-2 hours**
Elevation Gain	**1,100 ft**
High Point	**7,200 ft**
Physical Difficulty	■■
Technical Difficulty	■■
Terrain	**Trail**

Access from Canyon and Broadway Drive south on Broadway to the intersection of Hwy 93 and Hwy 6 at a traffic light in Golden. Bear left and then turn right at the second traffic light you come to, which is Jefferson County Parkway (23.3 miles from Boulder). Following the signs for Morrison and I-70, drive 1 mile to Apex Park, marked by a small brown sign on the right side of the road. The park is next to Heritage Square.
Drive Time 30 minutes

The Ride Begin on the Apex Trail. Ride across a meadow and climb through a challenging, narrow, rock walled section. Intersect the Sledge Trail and turn right, climbing steeply up this rocky single track. At the top of the climb, bear right on the Grubstake Loop Trail. As you pedal around Indian Mountain there is a panorama of the Front Range stretching from Red Rocks, across Denver, to Golden. Switchback up the back side of Indian Mountain. Lookout Mountain is above you. Continue straight past the Bonanza Trail and turn left on the Pick Trail. Turn right on the Sledge Trail, then left on the Apex Trail and return to the start.

Trail Notes The Apex Trail offers a relatively uncrowded, good, quick workout near Boulder. For a longer ride, you could do the loop twice or combine it with one of the other nearby Open Space Park trails. This is a popular trail with hikers; be on the lookout.

31

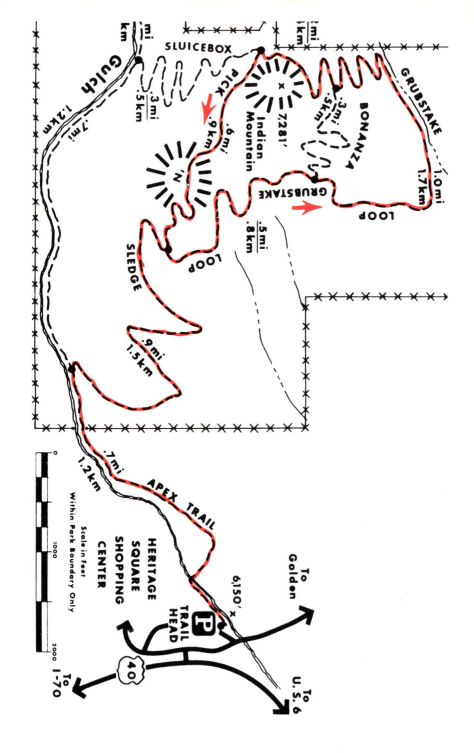

SLUICEBOX

Gulch

.7mi
1.2km

km

mi

.3mi
.5km

PICK

.9km

.6mi

Indian
Mountain

7,281'

N

GRUBSTAKE

.5km
.3mi

BONANZA

1.7km
1.0mi

LOOP

GRUBSTAKE

.5mi
.8km

LOOP

SLEDGE

.9mi
1.5km

APEX TRAIL

.7mi
1.2km

HERITAGE
SQUARE
SHOPPING
CENTER

6,150'

To
Golden

TRAIL
HEAD

P

To
U.S. 6

40

To
I-70

Scale in Feet
Within Park Boundary Only

0

1000

2000

32

15 **Caribou Road**

Distance	**11.8 miles**
Time	**2-3 hours**
Elevation Gain	**1,650 ft**
High Point	**6,650 ft**
Physical Difficulty	◆
Technical Difficulty	■
Terrain	**2WD Road**

Access from Canyon and Broadway Drive west on Canyon (Hwy 119) to Nederland. Bear left on Hwy 119 and take your first right into a public parking lot.
Drive Time 25 minutes

The Ride From the lot, turn left on Hwy 72 East and ride .4 miles to a green sign for Caribou on the left side of the road. Turn left and begin climbing dirt Forest Service Road 108. At .8 miles, stay left and continue climbing. Stay on the main road all the way up. At a three-way intersection with FS 506, bear left on Road 108. Climb past the Caribou silver mine and an old stone building. This route ends at the intersection with the Rainbow Lakes Road (FS 505). Return as you came.

Trail Notes Caribou was once a mining camp serving what was then called the world's richest silver mill. In fact, Colorado was nicknamed the Silver State because of the Caribou find. When the silver market collapsed in 1893, Caribou went the way of the dinosaur and all that remains are two dilapidated buildings and a vandalized cemetery above the old town-site.

33

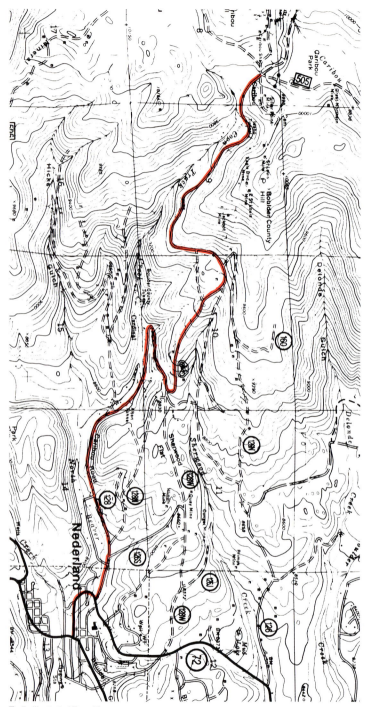

Trails Illustrated Topo Maps

34

Distance	**11.4 miles**
Time	**1.5-2.5 hours**
Elevation Gain	**1,500 ft**
High Point	**10,200 ft**
Physical Difficulty	◆
Technical Difficulty	■■
Terrain	**2WD Road**

Access from Canyon and Broadway Drive west on Canyon (Hwy 119) to Nederland. From Nederland, bear left on 119 for .6 miles to BC 130, the road to Eldora. Stay right at a turn-off for the Eldora Ski Area, continue 2.5 miles to the stop sign at 6th St. in the town of Eldora and park off the road.
Drive Time 35 minutes

The Ride Ride up the Eldora road to the end of the pavement and continue on the dirt. Stay right at a turn-off for Hessie and climb more steeply. Stay on the main road at all junctions. Pass several houses, following the South Fork of Upper Boulder Creek, which resembles a shallow gorge in places. Reach the 4th of July Campground at 5.7 miles and return as you came.

Trail Notes The 4th of July Road is a scenic route to a campground at the Indian Peaks Wilderness boundary. Bikes are not allowed in the wilderness area beyond the campground, but you can hike from there. The town of Eldora boomed in the 1890s when gold was discovered nearby. At the time, Nederland was suffering the effects of the collapse of the silver market so the gold strike was a boon to the local economy. However, the discovery was small and the rush lasted less than ten years leaving Eldora a ghost town until it was revived by the opening of the Eldora Ski Area in 1962.

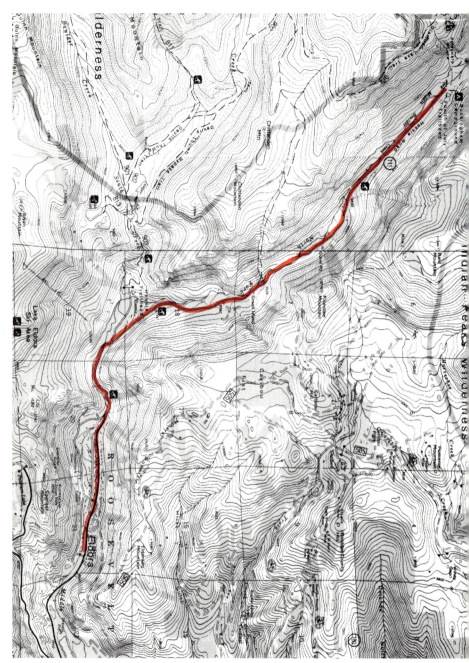

Trails Illustrated Topo Maps

17 **Red Rocks Trail**

Distance	**6 miles**
Time	**1-2 hours**
Elevation Gain	**1,100 ft**
High Point	**6,950 ft**
Physical Difficulty	■■
Technical Difficulty	◆
Terrain	**Trail**

Access from Canyon and Broadway Drive south on Broadway to the intersection of Hwy 93 and Hwy 6 at a traffic light in Golden. Bear left and then turn right at the second traffic light, which is Jefferson County Parkway (23.3 miles from Boulder). Follow the signs for Morrison and I-70, drive under I-70 and turn right into Matthews/Winters Park, marked by a brown sign.
Drive Time 35 minutes

The Ride Ride out of the parking lot, cross the highway and join the dirt road on the other side. Climb past a gate and turn right on the Dakota Ridge Trail. Follow this technical trail as it climbs and descends along the Hogback and ends at the bottom of a staircase on a paved road. Cross the road, go right, behind a yellow cement barricade and rejoin the trail on your left. Climb briefly and then descend sharply to the highway. Control your speed at the bottom; the trail dumps right onto the highway! Cross the highway, enter Red Rocks Park and turn right on the Red Rocks Trail. Cross several dirt roads and ride to an intersection with the Morrison Slide Trail. Turn right, ride just under 1 mile and intersect the Slide Trail again. Stay right, ride to the Village Walk Trail, turn right and return to the start.

Option Two Upon intersecting the Morrison Slide Trail for the second time, turn left on it and climb several steep switchbacks to a view point. Follow a very challenging, switchbacking descent leading you back to the intersection with the Red Rocks Trail. Go straight on the Red Rocks Trail, retracing your path to the Morrison Slide Trail. At the Slide Trail, bear right, continue to the Village Walk Trail, turn right and return to the start.

Trail Notes The Dakota Ridge Trail is an early season ride. It can be very sandy, especially after dry weather or later in the season when it has been ridden a lot. The optional Morrison Slide Trail Loop is tough and has some steep drop-offs, ride with caution. The Red Rocks Trail is often very crowded. Ride in control and yield to others.

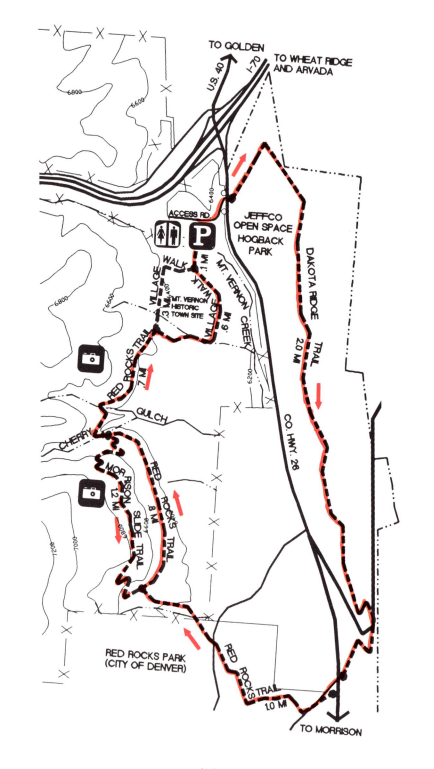

TO GOLDEN

TO WHEAT RIDGE
AND ARVADA

U.S. 40

I-70

6800

6600

ACCESS RD.

P

JEFFCO
OPEN SPACE
HOGBACK
PARK

DAKOTA RIDGE TRAIL

2.0 M

VILLAGE WALK .1 M

MT. VERNON CREEK

VILLAGE WALK

.9 M

MT. VERNON
HISTORIC
TOWN SITE

.3

6600

6800

6400

6200

6000

RED ROCKS TRAIL

.7 M

GULCH

CHERRY

MORRISON SLIDE TRAIL

1.2 M

RED ROCKS TRAIL

.8 M

5800

6600

CO. HWY. 26

7200

7000

6800

RED ROCKS PARK
(CITY OF DENVER)

RED ROCKS TRAIL

1.0 M

TO MORRISON

38

18 Buchanan Pass Trail

Distance	**6 miles**
Time	**1.5-2.5 hours**
Elevation Gain	**650 ft**
High Point	**9,400 ft**
Physical Difficulty	■
Technical Difficulty	◆◆
Terrain	**Trail**

Access Drive west on Canyon (Hwy 119) to Nederland. Bear right on Hwy 72 East and continue 18 miles to Peaceful Valley. Turn left, following a sign for a National Forest Recreation Area and drive to the parking area at the end of the road, just past the Camp Dick camp ground.
Drive Time 50 minutes

The Ride Go through the gate at the end of the road, following the signs for Buchanan Pass and the St. Vrain Trail. Take your first right on the Buchanan Pass Trail. Cross a bridge and continue up the trail, navigating through a series of obstacles, including logs, rocks and stream crossings. Stay left at a junction with a horse trail. Arrive at Timberline Falls at 2.3 miles. At 3 miles, come to a log bridge and return as you came.

Trail Notes The Buchanan Pass Trail is more of a trials course than a trail. The technical challenges are not super-difficult but are relentless. You can continue up the trail for several more miles if you'd like. The trail should only be ridden later in the spring after the run-off has subsided and it has dried out.

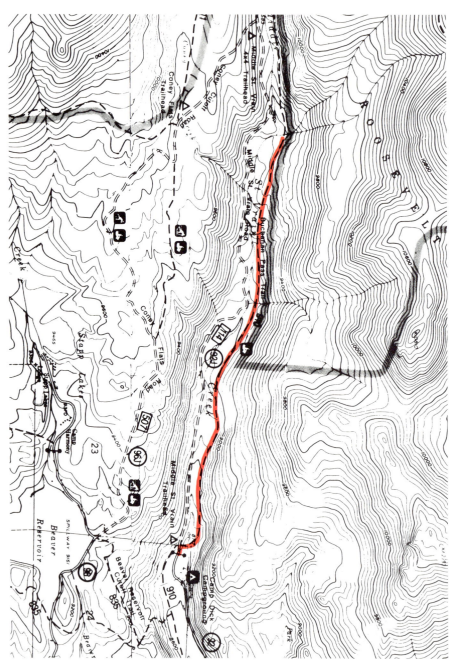

Trails Illustrated Topo Maps

40

E
L
E 7500
V 7000
A 6500
T 6000
I   0 1 2 3 4 5 6 7 8 9 10
O   M I L E S
N

Distance	**9.5 miles**
Time	**1.5-2.5 hours**
Elevation Gain	**1,550 ft**
High Point	**7,500 ft**
Physical Difficulty	◆
Technical Difficulty	◆
Terrain	**2WD Road,**
	Trail

Access from Canyon and Broadway Drive 17.4 miles south on Hwy 93 (Broadway) to a White Ranch Open Space sign. Turn right on 56th St., drive 1 mile to the end of the road and turn right into the parking lot. **Drive Time** 25 minutes

The Ride Warm up as you climb gradually along the sandy Belcher Hill Trail. Ride down a set of stairs, cross a bridge and begin climbing more steeply up a loose dirt and rock road. Go straight at an intersection with the Longhorn Trail and continue up this difficult section of road. At a junction with the Mustang Trail go straight again. At a third junction, stay straight on the Belcher Hill Trail, which becomes single track. Climb one more steep section and descend to the upper parking lot. Cross the lot and join the Mustang Trail. Turn right on the Rawhide Trail and come to a second parking area. Continue along the Rawhide Trail, turn right on the Longhorn Trail and descend sharply. Pass the Maverick Trail and turn right on the Shorthorn Trail. Descend and climb back to the Longhorn Trail, go straight past the Mustang Trail, follow a short down-hill, turn left on the Belcher Hill Trail and return to the start.

Option 1 At the top of the Belcher Hill Trail, turn left on the Mustang Trail and descend steeply on this occasionally technically challenging trail. Ride past the Sawmill and Belcher Hill Trails to an intersection with the Longhorn Trail. Turn right, descend to the Belcher Hill Trail, turn left and return to the start.

Trail Notes White Ranch has tough climbs and great descents. The park is very popular but is large enough that people get spread out. Control your speed on the narrow descents to avoid collisions. This trail is much more fun to ride early in summer or any time when there has been some rain, as it tends to get sandy later in the season. The Mustang Trail Option is less crowded than other trails in the park.

41

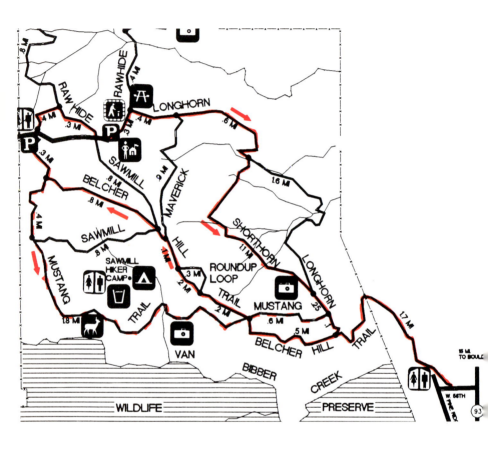

Distance	**9 miles**
Time	**1.5-2.5 hours**
Elevation Gain	**1,450 ft**
High Point	**7,500 ft**
Physical Difficulty	◆
Technical Difficulty	◆
Terrain	**2WD Road, Trail**

ELEVATION

7500
7000
6500

0 1 2 3 4 5 6 7 8 9
M I L E S

Access from Canyon and Broadway Ride or drive south on Broadway to Baseline, turn right and continue 10.7 miles, up and over Flagstaff Mountain and turn left on Pika Road. In .7 miles, turn right and downhill. In .4 more miles, turn right on Eldorado Canyon Trail and park in the lower Walker Ranch lot.
Drive Time 30 minutes

The Ride Ride back up to the paved Flagstaff Road. Carefully turn left onto it and ride .5 miles to the upper Walker Ranch parking lot. Ride through the lot, join the South Boulder Creek Trail and cruise down this easy, wide path to South Boulder Creek. Cross the bridge and join the Crescent Meadows Trail. The climb is long and tough and some sections are so technical that "you'd have to be Hans Rey to ride them," as my friend C.J. puts it. At an intersection with a road, turn left, rejoin the sin-gletrack, climb briefly and then descend radically on another, rowdy, technical section with steep rock shelves and drop-offs. Walk down to South Boulder Creek on an unrideable, steep, rocky trail. Watch your traction if you have cleated shoes! Turn right at the creek and walk to a bridge. Cross the river and climb steeply out of the drainage on an old jeep road. At an intersection with the Columbine Gulch Trail, stay right and return to the start.

Trail Notes This route is described as starting at the lower parking lot so you get the long climb on the road out of the way at the start. Walker Ranch, being the best known trail in Boulder, gets major pressure. The Boulder County Parks Department have even talked about closing it to bikes in the past. With the help of the Boulder Off-Road Alliance, we've been given a reprieve, but it's crucial that everyone be on their best bik-ing behavior to avoid conflicts with other trail users and to help keep the trail open to everyone.

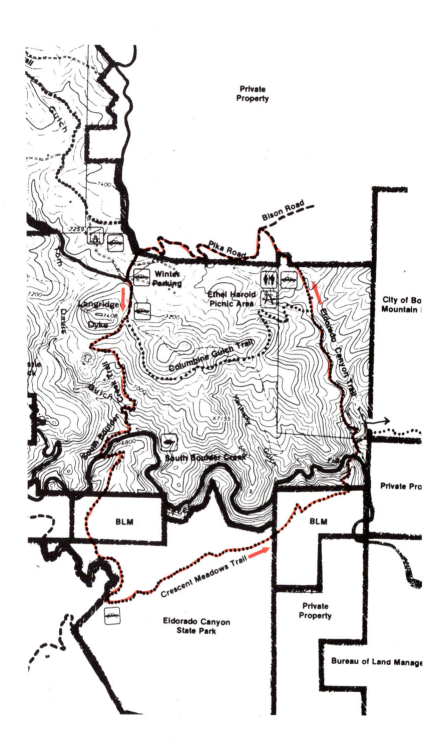

Private
Property

Bison Road

Pika Road

Winter
Parking

Ethel Harold
Pichic Area

City of Bo
Mountain

Langridge
Dyke

Eldorado Canyon Trail

Columbine Gulch Trail

South Boulder

South Boulder Creek

Private Pro

BLM

BLM

Crescent Meadows Trail

Private
Property

Eldorado Canyon
State Park

Bureau of Land Manage

44

21 St. Vrain Trail

Distance	**7.2 miles**
Time	**1-2 hours**
Elevation Gain	**950 ft**
High Point	**8,700 ft**
Physical Difficulty	◆
Technical Difficulty	◆
Terrain	**Trail**

ELEVATION

9000
8500
8000

0 1 2 3 4 5 6 7 8

M I L E S

Access from Canyon and Broadway Drive 3.4 miles north on Broadway to Lee Hill Road, turn left and drive 6 miles to Sunshine Canyon Road. Turn right, drive 1 mile and turn left on Left-Hand Canyon Drive. Drive 3 miles to Jamestown and continue another 6.8 miles to the signed St. Vrain Trail. Turn right and park at the trailhead.
Drive Time 45 minutes

The Ride Start on a single track and follow it upstream along St. Vrain Creek. Where the trail intersects the creek, take the uphill left on a steep, rocky jeep road. At the top of the climb, turn left on a single track. The trail forks immediately. Turn left again and climb to the end of the trail at a dirt road. Turn right and descend to an intersection with several other roads. Take the third road from the left and descend on this very rocky, technically challenging road before climbing back to the point where you turned onto the single track above St. Vrain Creek. Descend to St. Vrain Creek, rejoin the St. Vrain Trail and return to the start.

Trail Notes This is just one possible loop in the area. From the end of the St. Vrain Trail there is a network of overgrown jeep roads used primarily by mountain bikers and moto-crossers. This area abuts several tracts of private land and some of the roads end abruptly. You probably couldn't get too lost exploring the area as there are only several miles of road but all the intersecting trails can be confusing.

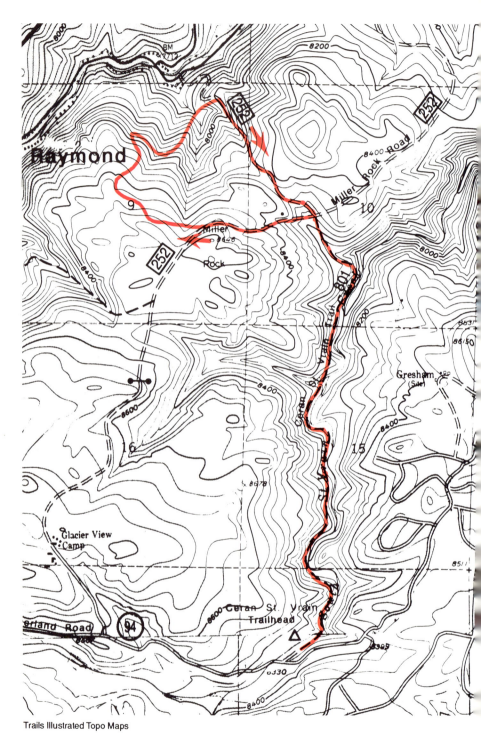

Trails Illustrated Topo Maps

46

22 Eldorado Mountain Trail

Distance	**15.9 miles**
Time	**3-5 hours**
Elevation Gain	**1,900 ft**
High Point	**10,150 ft**
Physical Difficulty	◆
Technical Difficulty	◆
Terrain	**Paved Road**
	2WD, 4WD Road

Access from Canyon and Broadway Take Canyon (Hwy 119) west to Nederland, bear left on Hwy 119, take your first right and park in the public parking lot.
Drive Time 25 minutes

The Ride From the lot, turn left on Hwy 72 east and ride .4 miles to a green sign for Caribou on the left side of the road. Turn left and climb dirt Forest Service Road 108. At .8 miles, stay left and continue climbing. Stay on the main road all the way up. At a three-way intersection with FS 506, continue straight on Road 108. Climb past the Caribou silver mine and an old stone building. Continue past an intersection with the Rainbow Lakes road and take your next left, climbing past an old cabin, up a very steep, rocky 4WD road. Cross a meadow, following the main road at all junctions. At an intersection with a good road on your left, stay straight. The route heads into the forest and alternately climbs and descends toward Eldora. As the road comes out of the forest it drops sharply and is technical shelf rock. Ride into the town of Eldora, turn left on Main St., ride to Hwy 119, turn left again and return to Nederland.

Trail Notes The Eldorado Mountain Trail is a physically and technically challenging loop passing three of the most important former mining camps in the Boulder area. I have only done this loop once and I did it the opposite way from what I have described here. I tried to do it again several times last spring but was turned back by snow. The route is fairly obvious, but you are on your own. If you follow the main road, heading toward Eldora at every intersection, you'll be fine; it's not very hard to find.

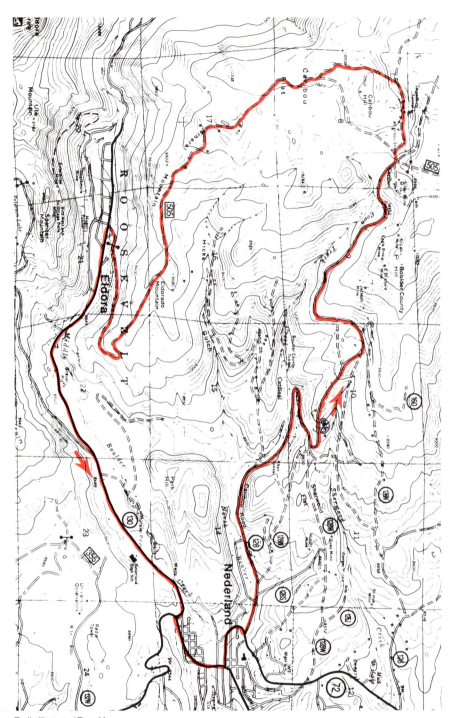

Trails Illustrated Topo Maps

48

M I L E S

Distance	27 miles
Time	4-6 hours
Elevation Gain	2,800 ft
High Point	10,550 ft
Physical Difficulty	◆
Technical Difficulty	◆◆
Terrain	**Paved Road, Dirt Road, Trail**

Access from Canyon and Broadway Drive west on Canyon (Hwy 119) to Nederland. In Nederland, turn right on Hwy 72 East, toward Ward. Drive 18 miles to Peaceful Valley and turn left on a dirt road marked with a National Forest Recreation Sign. Drive to the end of the road, just past Camp Dick, and park in a dirt lot by a gate.
Drive Time 50 minutes

The Ride Pedal back out to Hwy 72, turn right and ride 12 miles up the highway to a sign for the C.U. Research Station (FS 298). Turn right on the dirt road and ride .4 miles to the Sourdough trailhead, on your right. Turn onto the Sourdough Trail and climb this well-marked, rocky single track. The climb is 4 miles long and reaches 10,400 before descending to the paved Brainard Lake Road. Cross the road and continue descending along a very rocky, technically challenging section. Climb a brief, steep hill and descend to the Beaver Reservoir Road. Continue on the Sourdough Trail. At a junction with a horse trail, stay left and follow the trail back to the start at Peaceful Valley.

Trail Notes The Sourdough Trail can be ridden one way by shuttling a second car to the C.U. Research station. However, the paved, 12 mile road section only takes about an hour and is not very difficult. Hwy 72 gets little traffic and has very wide shoulders; it's ideal for road riding. Allow plenty of time to do the ride. The single track is mostly downhill but there are some slow, rocky, technically demanding sections below Brainard Lake. Because of the high altitude, the trail is best ridden in summer and early fall. I have been turned around by snow in early June and October.

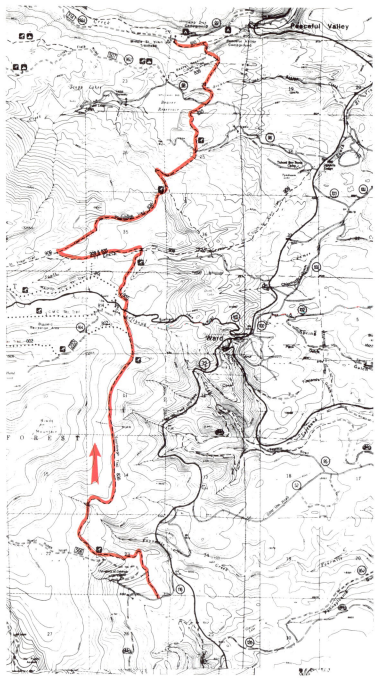

Trails Illustrated Topo Maps

Maverick Trail

Distance	**15.5 miles**
Time	**3-4.5 hours**
Elevation Gain	**3,000 ft**
High Point	**7,750 ft**
Physical Difficulty	◆◆
Technical Difficulty	◆◆
Terrain	**2WD Road, Trail**

Access from Canyon and Broadway Drive 17.4 miles south on Hwy 93 (Broadway), to a sign for White Ranch Open Space. Turn right on 56th St., drive 1 mile to the end of the road and turn right into the parking lot. **Drive Time** 25 minutes

The Ride Beginning on the Belcher Hill Trail, climb to its intersection with the Longhorn Trail and turn right. Stay right at an intersection with the Mustang Trail and right again at the Shorthorn Trail. Descend and climb along this technically and physically demanding trail to its end at the Shorthorn Trail. Pass the Maverick Trail again, stay left at an intersection with the Rawhide Trail and come to the upper parking lot. Go through the lot and turn right at the second Rawhide trail sign, at the far end of the lot by a gate. Descend along this dirt road, pass a single track and continue on the Rawhide Trail. Continue past the Wrangler's Run Trail and climb to the Waterhole Trail. About 100 yards up the Waterhole Trail is a pump if you need water. If not, stay on the Rawhide Trail. The trail becomes a great single track, climbing through a pine forest, then descending past the Waterhole and Wrangler's Run Trails again. The trail becomes more technical beyond the Wrangler's Run Trail. Retrace your route through the parking lot, descend briefly and turn left on the first single track you come to. Climb to another parking lot, cross it and climb to a junction with the Mustang Trail. Turn right and descend steeply past the Belcher Hill and Sawmill Trails. Climb to an intersection, cross the Belcher Hill Trail again and continue on the Mustang. At the Longhorn Trail, turn right and coast down to the Belcher Hill Trail. Turn left on this dirt road and return to the start.

Trail Notes Walker Ranch is a long, physically and technically challenging tour for expert riders in good shape. The pump at the Waterhole Trail runs from spring until fall so water is not a problem, but bring some food as the route is hot and tiring. Walker Ranch is very popular; be on the look out for other trail users.

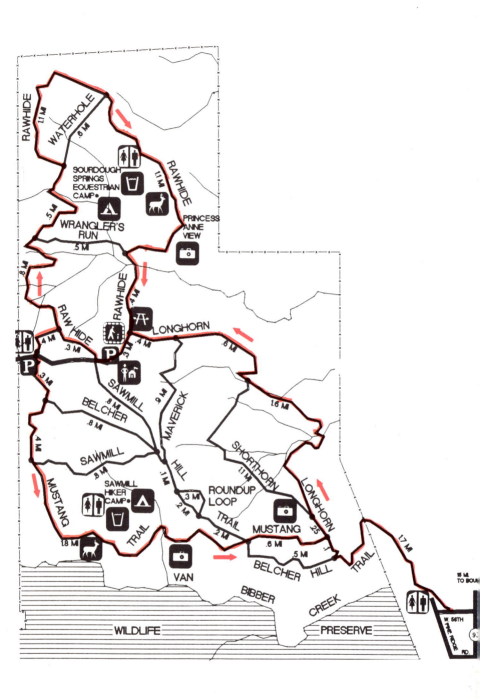

RAWHIDE

WATERHOLE
1.1 MI
.6 MI

RAWHIDE
1.1 MI

SOURDOUGH
SPRINGS
EQUESTRIAN
CAMP

PRINCESS
ANNE
VIEW

.5 MI

WRANGLER'S
RUN

.5 MI

.8 MI

RAW HIDE

RAWHIDE
.4 MI

.8 MI

LONGHORN

.4 MI

.6 MI

.4 MI

.3 MI

P

.3 MI

P

SAWMILL

.8 MI

BELCHER

.8 MI

.4 MI

SAWMILL

.9 MI

MAVERICK

1.6 MI

SHORTHORN

LONGHORN

.8 MI

SAWMILL
HIKER
CAMP

HILL

1.1 MI

1 MI

ROUNDUP
LOOP

MUSTANG

.3 MI

.2 MI

TRAIL

.25

MUSTANG

.6 MI

1.8 MI

TRAIL

.2 MI

.1

.5 MI

1.7 MI

VAN

BELCHER   HILL   TRAIL

15 MI
TO BOU

BIBBER

CREEK

W. 56TH

PRESERVE

W. 56TH
PINE RIDGE
RD

9

WILDLIFE